Turn Your Dissertation into a Book

TURN YOUR DISSERTATION INTO A BOOK

CONSTANCE BRITTAIN BOUCHARD

Daimbert Publishing Enterprises

www.Daimbert.com

ISBN 979-8859972036

First ebook edition March 2023

First printing September 2023

Contents

Chapter 1

Do you Need a Book?

You finished your dissertation. You successfully defended and are now a PhD (Piled Higher and Deeper) rather than an ABD (Alienated, Broke, and Depressed). You probably know more about your dissertation topic and care less than anyone else on the planet. And yet they now expect you to turn it into a book?

Okay, you don't have to turn it into a book right away, if indeed ever. Spend six months thinking about something else (maybe your second big project?). When you go back and look at your dissertation, it may surprise you by looking like something written by a smart person (which of course it was). Now is the time (six months post-defense) to decide if the dissertation should become a book or if it would work better as a series of articles.

If there's an overall argument that builds as you go along, then it's a book (or proto-book). If each chapter is about something different, all interesting and sort-of related, but each capable of standing by itself, its future is a series of articles. Even for something that may become a book, there's often a topic that didn't quite fit with the rest of the argument, or one you wished you could explore more but didn't have time to explore before the defense, and such topics can be their own articles.

Don't feel you absolutely must write a book if your dissertation resists becoming one. Among academic historians, even those who are able to make a career of it, half never publish a book. Most colleges and universities, even a lot of elite ones, will treat a series of fine articles as the equivalent of a book. And among those historians who do produce a book, half only ever write a single one, often late in their career.

Or suppose you are *through* with academe and are going to sell insurance or join your Mom's company as a junior vice president.   In that case you may have no interest in ever thinking about your dissertation again and cringe when you realize that your university has put it in their library and has also "helpfully" deposited it on some site so that people in the future can read it.

Just don't let your dissertation vanish in the haze. If there's any chance you may want to publish it (or parts of it), do so soon.   Or at least get started.   It is very sad when someone writes a   solid dissertation, forgets about it for a dozen years, and then tries to get back to it.   They've been teaching at an elite high school or at an undergraduate college where research isn't valued, or at a series of universities as they try to cobble a living together as an adjunct, or have been selling insurance.   But they still think writing a book (or at least some articles) would be nice.   They apply for a grant for some free time to get to work.   But the granting agency is not impressed with a proposal that addresses questions that were interesting questions a dozen years ago, but have largely been answered now, accompanied by a bibliography at least a decade out of date.

Seems like you're stuck with it. At least think about writing that book, even if you eventually decide that articles would be a better way to go, even if Mom's company would pay far, far better than anything in academe. This guide is intended to help you write it. I'm a historian, so I address the issues with a historian's perspective, but most of my comments apply equally well to other "book disciplines" in the humanities and social science, including English, political science, anthropology, and so on.

So get past the stage of fear and loathing. You successfully defended your dissertation! It's already well on the way to becoming a book. All you have to do is leave out the parts you don't need, put in the parts you should have, and refine your arguments. Easy! Let's get started.

Chapter 2
The Book's Introduction

The Introduction is the single most important chapter in the book. It's the one that readers and reviewers will read most closely, it's the one where readers will decide if it's worth continuing to read, it's the one that will appear in the Look Inside for your book's listing on Amazon. Recall taking a graduate seminar (you must have taken quite a number). You read the Introduction of the assigned book carefully, did a fast grad-read of the middle chapters, and slowed down again for the Conclusion, right? The same approach will be taken with your book, so make sure all the points you want people to take away are there in the Introduction.

It is indispensable at the outset to determine for sure what your book is about. (And no, "My book is *about* 250 pages!" is not an adequate answer, though it is amusing.) My graduate students used to call this "secret theme," because the person writing had a general idea of the point all their information was supporting, but it often took others to tell them what argument they were actually making. All good books have a central argument, so you need to figure it out. Write the Introduction as though you knew what it was, write the rest of the book, and then come back and rewrite the Introduction.

Your central argument has to be new, which you doubtless realized when you lived in terror of going by the New Books table in the library and seeing a book by some famous scholar on exactly your topic. You cannot write a book whose main theme is, "Dr. ABC says, and I agree." But no idea is entirely new, and you don't want to claim that yours is. Instead find a way to suggest that no one has done exactly what you are doing, even though previous work suggests that your analysis is the next logical step.

Identifying your central argument has a certain

Goldilocks feel to it. It has to be narrow but not too narrow. That is, your Introduction should address a broad topic that many scholars are interested in, then indicate that your sources and your arguments are narrow enough to be contained within a 200-page book, yet broad enough in their implications that anyone researching the topic in general should be able to learn from it.

Throughout you need to make sure the book will be interesting to a wide range of readers, even while not making sweeping statements covering centuries (it is, after all, your first book). The goal is to focus enough on your topic that you can cover it all, while assuring that even those who may never use your sources in their own scholarship will want to read the book. You can do this. After all, you satisfied all the different members of your doctoral committee.

The central argument should appear in the first two or three pages of the book manuscript. You can either state it right up front, or you can start with an illustrative story/example and follow it (around p. 2) with the argument. If you start with an intriguing case (which a lot of publishers want you to do), then you also need a Preface that states your argument baldly, as well as thanking all the people who helped you. (It used to be thought amusing to say something like, "And I'd like to thank my wife, without whose help the book would have been written in half the time," but it isn't any more.)

There are several different ways to state your argument and develop it in the Introduction. The easiest is to give what we historians call a historiographic context (grossly simplified at this point), that is putting your work in the context of other scholarship. I'm paraphrasing here, so find your own wording, but you can say something like, "Scholars have long studied xyz," or "It is well known that xyz," and have a sentence or two on what xyz is. Then comes your "But" sentence. The two main choices are, "But they have never...." or "But the evidence suggests that, to the contrary...." So in just a single paragraph you can say what scholarly context your book is in and whether you are extending previous analysis beyond where it's gotten so far or are setting out to show that previous analysis is mistaken.

Example: You might say that a lot of intellectual historians have studied Thomas Aquinas, and a lot of social historians have studied thirteenth-century women, but no one has ever discussed the role of women in Aquinas's life (probably a bad example, but you get the point). This would be a book designed to extend previous analysis. You can make it sound as though this is the obvious next step for historians both of women and of Aquinas to take.

You can even make it sound as though you thoughtfully noticed this gap in the scholarship and decided it needed to be filled, and you are the person to do it, and the sources that you're using are exactly the ones to fill the gap. Now of course it didn't work that way. You had some ideas, you looked at some sources, the sources gave you new ideas, and you blundered your way into your dissertation topic. That's how everyone does it. But it's a polite fiction to allow the author to suggest they knew what they were doing from the beginning.

Alternately, you may want to plunge into some debate and argue that everyone in sight has gotten everything wrong and that only you can tell the true story. This is most definitely *not* recommended for a first book. Even if you think everyone is wrong, "there's a gap in previous scholarship" is a much better approach than "only I understand the issues." You can work in criticism of previous works as you go.

While setting out your argument, be sure to indicate the time period and the place your book will cover. No book can cover everything, so you need to narrow down your focus in both time and space. With luck, you can suggest that this particular focus is uniquely suited to address the larger questions that the book will answer.

As you state your book's major themes, also be sure to define any analytic terms you will be using throughout. This does not mean giving a dictionary definition, but rather giving a sense of how you will be using a particular word or phrase. You might be able to do so in a sentence, or it might take several paragraphs, but defining your terms early will make your book's argument much easier to follow.

Having set out your argument, the Introduction should next go to the sources. For a historian, this means the primary sources, those written at the time of the historical events being discussed. For other disciplines, it would be something comparable, literary works or field studies or whatever. The sources are the heart of your book and will determine its value. You need either to study sources that have been (at least relatively) neglected, or else (which is harder) have exciting new insights into sources previous scholars treated as thoroughly understood. So spend a good part of your Introduction talking about the nature of these sources.

For a historian, it's best if the sources be found at least in part in the archives. Published documents give you far fewer opportunities to come up with something new, because many other scholars have probably already looked them over. If you weren't able to get to the archives while writing your dissertation, see if you can get a travel grant to assist you in getting there now, as you start turning your dissertation into a book. More and more is available on-line, but a whole lot has never been digitized, and the original pieces of parchment or paper, those the scribe handled, will speak to you as an image on a screen never will.

After a thorough discussion of the sources, it's time to give an overview of the book's structure. Give a sentence or two to each chapter, suggesting how they tie together and build your argument. Having done so, restate your main argument, making it sound much more broadly relevant than the actual topic might suggest.

By the time someone has undertaken (one hopes) a careful reading of your Introduction, they should have an excellent idea of what arguments you intend to make, what kind of sources you will use to support the argument, and where the book fits into broader scholarship. A graduate student could even write a précis of your book from the Introduction.

But wait! you say. How can the Introduction fit the book into broader scholarship when we haven't even gotten to the Literature Review chapter? (what historians call the historiography chapter). Good news. You don't need that chapter! Then why, you say, did my committee require it?

Two reasons. The first is to make sure you actually became largely aware of where the field is and has been. No use announcing an exciting new methodological approach that everyone has actually been using for a decade. The other is to make sure you give credit where credit is due. Nothing a scholar hates more than to see a book right in her main field that doesn't seem to realize all she's done in that field. But now that you've done all of that to prove you can do it, no one wants you to recapitulate it all again.

Here Anglophone publishers are different from German ones. German dissertations (and first books) expect historians to include hundreds of pages of historiography, tracing how arguments have developed over the decades, citing everyone who's published on the topic. I've seen books by young German scholars with five hundred pages or more of historiography and a little over a hundred pages of original analysis. You don't have to do this. American and British academic presses in fact really really do not want you to do this.

You also do not want to do what French scholars often do, which is to summarize over many pages the current state of scholarship (or even the decades' old state of scholarship) on a topic as if they were going to agree with it, then suddenly start explaining that they are going to argue the exact opposite. This can look too much like self-contradiction. Always make clear who you are agreeing with and who disagreeing with, and do not waste your time disagreeing with a point of view that has had few supporters for a generation.

So what do you do with your Literature Review chapter? You break it up. If and when it appears, it will be in footnotes (or endnotes). You do not need to go back to nineteenth-century scholars and trace how your topic has been treated for a century and a half. Instead, you can make a fairly sweeping comment in the text about where the field is now, with a footnote that begins, "See, most recently..." or you can say something like, "Ever since this topic was first addressed by ...." and have a footnote to that scholarly pioneer, followed (same note) by the comment, "He was succeeded most notably by...." with a few standout names from the following decades (and I realize that the nineteenth-century pioneering scholar was almost certainly a He). Hold the number of footnotes down.

So there you are, with an Introduction. Time to get to the meat of the book.

Chapter 3
The Heart of the Book

The individual chapters will be a medley of discussion, analysis, and examples. As you go through, you will find spots where your committee made you put in material you yourself found irrelevant. Now is the time to take it back out. Other spots will seem oddly skimpy, the sections you never developed properly because you were running out of time. Work on those. But the main body of the book is up to you, with far less formal requirements for the structure and organization than in the Introduction.

When you were writing your dissertation, you doubtless had to check in regularly with your advisor, showing chapters in progress. Other members of your committee probably had something to say at various points, perhaps telling you one thing one month and the exact opposite the next. But at any rate you were subject to oversight. Now however you are really on your own. Your committee may make a few suggestions but they doubtless feel that at this stage their role has ended. Often a peer, someone working on their own book, can be very helpful. Read their draft in return. You can feel virtuous in reading and commenting on their manuscript even if you get nothing done on your own for three days. Besides, seeing the gaps in someone else's manuscript is a great way to reveal what may be lacking in yours.

There are several issues to keep in mind as you get started turning your dissertation into a book. Most importantly, find a safe path to follow between relying too much on other scholars and announcing that all other scholars are completely wrong. Your book should center on the contribution that you yourself are making. Too much attention to other scholars' work, either to agree or disagree with them, makes the book about them, whereas it should be about *your* ideas and your primary sources.

Think about what makes your book *different*. Throughout, you should not just repeat what is already known but make it clear that you are raising new arguments. You may be looking at new sources or providing new analysis or developing new approaches, but whatever it is, it is different from whatever has been done before. This is why your book is important. Embrace it.

To keep your book original, do *not* quote other scholars verbatim. Certainly you will cite them, certainly you will paraphrase them. But if your book has big block quotes throughout of other scholars with whom you agree, it will look like little more than a pastiche, or as I have heard it described, a miracle of modern pedantry. The reader may even wonder why they should bother reading your book, when everything useful has clearly been said already. In short, don't go there.

Now in fact there are a few situations in which you will want to give an exact quote. Sometimes a scholar has stated something so clearly and elegantly that you couldn't say it better yourself. This is especially the case when someone has come up with a definition of an analytic term or of a theoretical construct, and their definition has become a classic. But in this case you may find that you need quote only a few words, or at most a sentence.

The one time that you *do* want to quote someone fairly extensively is if you're going to disagree with them. This is to make it clear that you are not mischaracterizing what they said, and they really did make such an inane statement. But be careful about being too argumentative with people who have been in the field a lot longer than you have. You do not have to defer to their position, but you don't want to seem nasty either. The footnotes are often a good place to throw shade on others' misguided conclusions.

Sometimes another scholar will have come to the same conclusion on some point as you did, probably before you did, but you worked it out yourself before reading their article. In this case a footnote is your friend. "A similar point is made by Scholar ABC," your note reads.

An amateurish looking footnote (hence something you want to avoid) is one that cites a source (usually a primary source), then adds, "As quoted in ...." giving a reference to a modern book or article. If you think a primary source makes a good point, go look at it yourself. Don't take another scholar's word for it saying what you want it to say. For one thing, in my experience modern scholars usually quote the part that is most useful for their argument, whereas for your purposes something more interesting may be in the next section. And you don't want to give the impression that you consulted something you didn't. In the rare case that the other scholar cites some source you just can't access (like an eighteenth-century edition of a thirteenth-century document, where the document is long lost and the edition exists only in a few copies in obscure libraries), you can just cite the secondary author.

By the way, it's easiest to put your footnotes in the right format as you go, rather than trying to convert them all at the end, which can be mind-deadening. Use whatever is the standard footnote style for your discipline. Chicago style is always safe. Unlike journals, which each have their own (somewhat idiosyncratic) way of doing notes, most presses can be persuaded that the style you're following is fine, as long as you're consistent.

As you style your footnotes, build your bibliography. Footnote format and bibliography format are different, as the *Chicago Manual of Style* makes clear. Why is this? you ask. Is it just to make the young scholar suffer as her predecessors had to suffer? Maybe. But the bibliography should not be neglected. Sometimes a press will suggest you don't need a bibliography, but pay this no mind. When someone first picks up your book, they will turn at once to the Bibliography. This immediately gives a sense of the evidentiary and scholarly base of your book. It will also assure Dr. ABC that you had the good sense to include his analysis.

When putting your book into the context of others' scholarship, be sure to *never* say something like, "Scholar ABC says this, while Scholar DEF says that, but the truth lies somewhere in between." This is flaccid and weak. The truth rarely lies somewhere in between. One may be right and the other wrong or, and this is a good argument if you can make it, both ABC and DEF have been asking the wrong questions. Search your manuscript for uses of the phrase "lies somewhere in between" to make sure you eliminate all of them.

Although you do not want more than a very minimal number of quotes from modern scholars, you will want to quote frequently from your primary sources.

Such quotations are used to support your arguments. As such, it is necessary always to put these quotations into context. The primary source cannot be expected to "speak for itself." First say what the quote is going to say, then give the quote, then discuss the quote and its implications. A good rule of thumb is that the discussion of a primary source quote should be as long as the quote itself, or longer.

As you present your arguments, try to have good, concrete examples. Even if you rely to a large extent on data sets or the acts of people in groups, a paragraph or two about individuals, here and throughout your discussion, will illustrate your points with a human touch that will make your book much more accessible. Just as publishers hate jargon, they hate works that are too theoretical and abstract.

Think not just about your overall argument but about your paragraphs. Avoid paragraphs that run a whole page, as they become hard to read. Two or three paragraphs a page will work, and you can have even shorter paragraphs. Make sure every paragraph has a good topic sentence. Remember how much you liked topic sentences when doing a grad-read of a book and hopping through it paragraph to paragraph. The topic sentence doesn't always have to be the first sentence, but the paragraph should be structured so that the grad student's eye is drawn right to it.

The chapters into which your book is divided will each have a title, not just be called "Chapter 1" or whatever. Try to avoid cutesy titles like "Love's Labour Lost." Rather, give the chapters titles that reflect the content. If you do this right, someone just looking at the chapter titles in the Table of Contents will be able to get a decent sense of how you build your argument.

As you write your chapters, think about what order would be best, which may not match the order in your dissertation. Within the chapters, it's usually best to have subsections, each with their own subheading. Each subsection functions as its own mini-chapter, starting with a paragraph that says what you will discuss in this section, and a paragraph at the end that pulls it together and aims the reader toward the next subsection. These comments throughout are often called "signposting," and publishers like them because they make it easier to follow the argument. Graduate students like them because it makes a grad-read easier. (Think about what you liked in an assigned book in graduate seminar, and writing your own book will become much more straightforward.)

Graduate students and other scholars are, most likely, your primary audience, but as you write keep in mind that you also want to make your book accessible to the non-specialist reader. The History Bookclub has long had many faithful readers who enjoy reading non-fiction in areas outside their own, including biologists, engineers, and people selling insurance. Other disciplines also attract interested non-specialists. Try to write clearly and engagingly enough that such readers will want to read the book and be able to follow your arguments. Even Mom may actually read it, not just put it on a shelf. If you can manage to do this, your book may end up in public libraries and big bookstores, rather than just in university libraries, even in graduate seminars.

As you decide what to include, what to expand, and what to leave out, you need to find a middle path (you've been seeing that advice from me a lot, haven't you). On the one hand, resist the urge to throw in every thought you've had, no matter how tangential. On the other hand, resist equally firmly the desire to "save" something for a later book. If it belongs in this book, put it in. You may never write a second book, and if you do it will probably be more than the unused portions of your dissertation.

This is your first book, and with luck it will turn out to be a good example of what a first book should be, relatively short, focused on a body of sources that you have come to know intimately, addressing a fairly narrow topic that has much broader implications.

With a second book you can spread out more, but you don't have to worry about that yet. Write *this* book.

As you write, make back-ups. This cannot be stressed too much. This is why God invented flash drives. If you back up every day, at most you'll lose a day's work. Files get corrupted. Laptops get stolen. I had an MA student who accidentally dumped a Big Gulp onto her laptop, with her MA thesis. Although she had a partial print out, the trauma kept her from ever finishing. Better have two back-up drives, one saved off-site. Drop Box and a file emailed to yourself, left sitting on the university server, can help. Even if you never need the back-up, it will keep you from moments of terror when you go to open your manuscript's file and your computer says, "What file can you mean?" (Show your computer the flash drive to jog its memory.)

Even though everything is electronic these days, print your chapters out periodically. Humans proof read better with paper than on a screen, and it may be easier to see how your material should be organized if you can spread out your pages and ponder different ways to order them. Your book is, after all, going to be a physical book (you hope), so getting a preview of your words on paper is often helpful.

At the end you need a Conclusion. The temptation is to write a very short conclusion, something like, "That's all, folks!" (not really, but you know what I mean). Or you might be thinking of something more like an Epilogue, what happened afterwards, or where research on this broad topic might go in the future. But no. You need a real conclusion. (You can slip your epilogue-ideas into the Conclusion.) Go back through all your chapters and remind yourself of the main points of each. Weave all these points together; don't just state them in order. Remember, the Conclusion is going to be the second most-read chapter in your book, after the Introduction, so you want readers to come away with a good understanding of your points.

Chapter 4
What Happens Next?

Get your book as good as you can make it. Polish it thoroughly, get all your footnotes in the right format, eliminate typos and sentences that make no sense and any Note to Self like "Insert analysis here." The ability to polish your prose easily was the goal when God invented word processors. Now you're ready to find a publisher.

The good news is that, statistically, it's far easier to find a good publisher for an academic book than for a novel, because there is far less competition. The further good news is that academic publishers actually care about the quality of their books and want them to be well received, even if they never become best-sellers. Now the academic publisher/university press would certainly like a best-seller, or at least a book that broke even, but their purpose in life is to publish good scholarly books. The bad news is that your book had therefore better be good.

Start by deciding what might be an appropriate press for you. Different university presses often have slightly different foci. In medieval studies, for example, the University of California Press has long published royal biographies, whereas the University of Pennsylvania Press has a number of titles addressing what might be considered more theoretical topics. Brill and Brepols (both based in Europe) will take books on an extremely narrow topic that American presses might not touch. These are of course generalities, and a good book may emerge from any press. But do enough research in recent titles to get a sense of which presses might be a good "fit" for your manuscript.

Now you have to persuade the editors of the press to find your book interesting. A press's website will tell you the names and contact information of the various editors. Different ones are responsible for different aspects of the press's line: for example, one may cover science books, another modern history, another literary studies, and so on. Your best bet is usually to meet the editor in person.

If there is a big conference in your field coming up, plan to go to it. The editor will probably be there too, both selling books and looking for new titles. Write the editor, tell her you are finishing a book on .... (insert about two sentences here), and ask if she would be free to meet at the conference. With luck, you may even have lunch bought for you as part of the meeting.

When talking to the editor (and it may just be over coffee or even just a discussion by the book display, don't feel neglected if you don't get a free lunch out of it, as she's got a lot of authors to meet) you need to have several different versions of the descriptions of your book all ready to go. First is the "elevator" as it has (rather awkwardly) come to be called, a description so short you could give it to someone while riding up to the third or fourth floor with them in an elevator. "My book will be the first to explore the women in Thomas Aquinas's life and the influence they had on him: his mother, his twin sister, and especially his landlady in Paris" (I'm just making up something here).

Then there's the somewhat longer version, about five minutes, that discusses how your book will be different from what else is out there, what your principal argument will be, and what sources you are using. Be clear about what time period, what place, and what approach. Be ready to answer questions on it, especially what makes it unlike previous scholarship. Don't feel compelled to try to impress the editor with your erudition. He already knows you're smart. You have a PhD and have written a book. He too probably has a PhD and may well have written a book. In particular don't use theoretical jargon in an ill-considered effort to impress. University presses hate jargon.

Now you may not be going to the meetings, or you

may not be able to meet with the editor, or the meet-ings may still be eight months off but you want to pitch your book *now*. That's fine. Email the editor instead. If she's interested, you can send her exactly what she would have asked you to send her if you and she had had a nice chat in the conference lunch room.

Note here that you can only send materials to one press at a time. It's a lot of work to assess an academic book, and no press wants to find out that they put in that work and then you say, Never mind, because your real First Choice was reading your submission at the same time and took the manuscript. You may want to publish through the press in the future, or the grumpy editor (made grumpy by you) may change positions and move to your First Choice press. You don't want to burn any bridges. One query at a time.

Once an editor expresses an interest in seeing more, start assembling your materials for the press. The editor will say what he wants, which is going to be some version of the following. Begin with a letter that describes your book in about a page and a half. Here include argument, geographic and temporal limits, and approximate length. Again, be clear how your book differs from what's already been said. Attach a table of contents for the whole book and a sample chapter, usually the Introduction. If the editor wants two chapters, attach the Introduction and the most interesting middle one.

If the editor likes what he sees, he will ask to see the complete manuscript. Send it to him, these days probably as a Word attachment to an email. (My first book was typed on a Selectric dancing-ball typewriter and mailed in, my second written on a computer main frame, printed out on paper with perforated edges and mailed in, the third written on a Mac and printed out on a laser printer and mailed in. My most recent was written on a Mac and emailed as an attachment. Technology has advanced.) If you don't *quite* have the manuscript ready for prime time, that's okay, just get it to the editor within the next few months, with a cover letter thanking him for his interest in your manuscript, which is now attached.

There will be some guidelines you'll have been sent about preparing your manuscript. You actually don't have to pay much attention to them. For example, the guidelines may suggest sending chapters as separate files. This doubtless dates from the era of floppy disks, when one disk couldn't hold very much. Put your whole book in one file, front matter through to the bibliography and appendixes. You don't want a chapter getting lost along the way! (I reviewed a book for a press once that had no Introduction but leapt straight into the discussion with no clue where we were going. When I asked about this, the press discovered they'd failed to send me that chapter. Whoops.)

The press will note how they want you to do your citations. You can ignore this too as long as you've followed a style that is appropriate for your discipline and is consistent throughout. If they really want notes done in a different format, you can change them later. The press will not reject your book because your initial submission used MLA rather than Chicago style (for example).

They may tell you to have the footnotes separate, at the end of each chapter or even at the end of the book. Most definitely do not do this. Your footnotes belong at the bottom of the page, as God intended. The suggestion that they go anywhere else doubtless dates from the days when text and notes were typeset separately on long sheets, then cut up and pasted onto pages to be "camera ready." Those days are gone. Your readers are going to be reading (most likely) a PDF on a screen and will either skip your excellent notes (if they are elsewhere) or become very grumpy, having to scroll back and forth. Happy readers are more important than some guidelines.

Oh, and don't have the footnotes in any smaller font than the main text. MS Word likes to shrink footnotes and put them in ugly font. Learn to use

Styles in Word, and set up a Style for your footnotes that gives them the same font and size and line spacing as the text. This makes things much easier for someone to read it. (The guidelines you got and ignored told you to double space. You can, but line-and-a-half spacing works just as well. I like 12-on-20, 12-point font, lines spaced 20 points apart. Just don't single space.)

Some new PhDs feel compelled to put a copyright slug, "Copyright © Your Name 2023." Resist the impulse. Under international law something you write is automatically copyrighted to you as soon as you finish it and make it available, so it's clearly and legally your book at this point. Putting in the copyright slug looks amateurish. Do you really think the press is going to steal your excellent ideas, publish them under a fake name, and rake in the millions? A little reality check might be in order. When it's time to publish the book, they will copyright it for you. You are licensing them your intellectual property (the book), and in return they will do all the hard work of getting it published, advertise it, make sure the relevant journals review it, and take it to conferences. They will even give you (some) money!

Once your manuscript is in the editor's hands, she will give it a quick read. If it's sloppy or incoherent or doesn't seem very interesting you will get a polite note saying it's not a good fit for their line at this time. (This is why you thoroughly polished your book before sending it out.) Resist the urge to write back and say that obviously the editor is incapable of recognizing quality. Recall my earlier comments about bridges and not burning them. Start querying a different press. But with luck the editor liked what she saw.

If so, she will send it to readers (also called reviewers), generally two, sometimes three. (If one reader of the original two loves it and the other hates it, two more may be asked for comments.) You can suggest reviewers, though the editor may not take your suggestions. You can also request that someone *not* review your manuscript. If you are arguing that Dr. ABC misunderstands a lot of important issues, and said ABC will probably not take this well, you can request that they not be a reviewer. Usually reviewers are chosen from people the press knows as reliable and conscientious, experts in the field. If you cite one scholar a lot, she may end up chosen as a reviewer.

Reviewers are incredibly important for your book. What they say will determine whether or not this press publishes your book and will help shape its final format. (You thought you were done writing with that last thorough polish? Sorry. You're not done.) You have to take them seriously because they are essentially doing it for free (or almost). The press may give them a couple hundred dollars for several weeks' worth of effort, so they wouldn't be doing it if they didn't think they were being helpful. You may or may not ever learn who they are, though if there's a quote on the back cover of your book once it's published that sounds a whole lot like one of the reviews, that's a clue. Another clue is if a reviewer says, "Clearly this author needs to read the new book by Dr. ABC, which will be out this coming summer."

The press will probably tell you to expect the reviews in a month to six weeks. Whatever they tell you, double it mentally. The reviewers are senior academics, teaching, grading papers, arguing with deans, and trying to write their own books. They want to help you but they're busy.

And then one day, when you've almost given up hope, or perhaps are thinking of something entirely different, the reviews arrive! I usually give them a quick look, get very grumpy and defensive, and put them aside until the next day, when I can look at them more dispassionately. Your goal is to learn how your book can be made even better by reading the reviews. Any temptation to say, "What nonsense! How can they be suggesting improvements when my book is already perfect?" must be resisted. Remember when you finished defending your dissertation and looked at it with ill-concealed loathing? Since when did it become perfect?

With luck the reviewers will all recommend publication, with revisions. It is extremely unlikely that they will recommend publication without further work. If the book has gotten as far as the editor requesting a complete manuscript and sending it out to reviewers, these reviewers will probably not recommend rejection. But it happens. If they do, carefully read through their comments, rewrite to take care of the problems they identify, and try another press.

So let's assume the readers recommend eventual publication. Pay attention to their suggestions, because the reviewers are all respected scholars who know what makes a good academic book. If they suggest incorporating books or articles you never heard of, find them and read them and work them into a footnote somewhere (or even lots of places). It may even be that those books or articles will make you rethink part of your approach. If the reviewers suggest you are arguing with a straw man or repeating your points unnecessarily combatively, you probably are. If they suggest you need to bring your points out more clearly in the Introduction, you probably do. If they suggest the book is longer than it needs to be, it probably is.

All that said, it's your book. You don't have to do every single thing the reviewers suggest. For one thing, they may contradict each other. But after reading and pondering their comments, the editor will expect you to make a "response." This is important. Your response, along with the readers' reports, are going to go to the press board, where they will decide whether or not to publish your book. You've come this close, don't lose it now.

Start your "response" with some statement that expresses gratitude to the close attention the readers gave your manuscript and their helpful suggestions. Spell out all the things you've decided to do to improve the book during final revisions, based on these suggestions. It's very important that everything about this response suggests you are a likable author who is easy to work with. Now you just have to figure out what to do about the comments that you really disagree with and have no intention of following.

If the readers contradict each other, you can easily say something like, "I was pleased to see Reader A praising me for writing in a jargon-free style, so I was somewhat surprised that Reader B thought I should include more on deconstructing the praxis of intersectionality. I believe in revising I can clarify the points s/he raised without resorting to jargon." (Remember, editors hate jargon.) This same approach, setting one reviewer off against another, can often get you out of having to agree to something you don't want to do.

Another good approach is to rephrase what the reader is asking you to do. Sometimes someone will insist you need to do xyz, but that's because they've misinterpreted your argument. In this case, if you restate the argument, the need to do what the reader is suggesting will disappear. So in your response you can say something like, "Reader A's real concern appears to be defg. I realize I may not have phrased my points clearly enough, as of course I never intended defg. When revised, the manuscript will clarify these points which, I trust, will address such concerns." You can think of other ways delicately to rephrase what is being asked of you into something you are happy to do.

After you send your "response" to the press (3-5 pages should do it, err on the shorter side), the editor will take the reviews, your response, and the manuscript to the press board. These are faculty members in book-centric disciplines, who may not be experts in your field but know academic books. They are generally guided by the editor. They meet every month or two to look at submissions, and they are the ones to make the final decision to publish.

So if the editor likes your book, the reviewers liked your book even though they had a lot of suggestions, and the press board liked your "response," they will offer you a contract. A book contract! Yes! They are really going to publish it. All you have to do is make all the changes you promised to make, do a final clean-up (and this time you really do have to follow the "guidelines," except for the part about separating the chapters into distinct files), and send the final version back to the press (MS Word file preferred).

Don't bother trying to negotiate over the contract they offer you. Academic books are rarely big money makers, so they aren't going to offer you an advance the way a New York publisher would for a book they expected to be popular. You'll probably make a few hundred dollars from the book, but if all you wanted was cash, it would have been a heck of a lot easier to flip burgers. In fact, the press may ask if your university can come up with a "subvention" to cover some of the cost of producing the book. If you've got a university position, it's always worth asking, but don't hold your breath. Scholarly societies also will sometimes pay for one or two subventions a year for first-time academic authors among their members.

At this stage, with a contract in hand, you can say the book is "in press." You have a contract, the press says they are going to publish it, it's definitely going to appear. You can even put "anticipated publication 2024" (or whenever) on your resume. Anticipate just under a year from when you send in the final revisions to when the book emerges hot off the presses. Colleges and universities that expect a book for tenure are generally satisfied with a copy of the contract.

It's extremely tacky however (not to say a lie) to suggest that your book is "in press" before you have a contract. Having a copy of the manuscript inside the press building does *not* count. You can say in a cover letter when applying for an academic position that you are turning (or even have turned) your dissertation into a book manuscript and have submitted it to a press (assuming you have), but don't name the press (unless specifically asked) and certainly don't put it on your resume. Nothing says "padded resume" louder than books and articles "in preparation" or "submitted."

The contract will usually give you a date six months in the future by which time they want the final manuscript. Try to meet this deadline, but most certainly do not cut corners in order to do so. Academic presses are used to academics. We are always running behind. (There's a reason we have no patience with our students turning in papers late. A Little Voice in the back of our heads says, "It would be *bad* if Someone didn't meet the deadline." We then chide the student. The Voice says, "Huh, that didn't work.")

You don't even have to apologize if the manuscript is a few months late. For six months late, apologize. If it's going to be a year, warn the editor, tell her you're still working on it but ran into issues (like moving, starting a new job, getting married or having children, all valid excuses). The editor would rather have a high-quality manuscript than just something that meets a deadline. They won't forget you have a contract.

One of the biggest challenges is going to be how to make the book shorter. The contract will most likely say something about 80,000 words, and yes, that includes footnotes and bibliography (MS Word will tell you how many words you have). But how, you say, can you leave out any of your most excellent prose? Well, remember when the longest thing you'd ever written was a 65-page MA thesis, and you looked at doctoral dissertations in your department, and the *short* ones were 200 or 300 pages, and you thought, "I can't do that"? But you did. And you can make your book shorter.

Start with the remnants of the Literature Review chapter. Yes, I know, you said you'd gotten rid of it, but bits are still there. Any book from before 1970 can be dispensed with, with extremely few exceptions (Marc Bloch and Georges Duby in medieval history).

A great many books from before 1990 or 2000 can be dispensed with. You may still want to have a footnote mention to someone, but unless their work is directly relevant to what you're arguing now, you don't need to summarize or discuss them.

Then start looking for repetition. Sure, you have to do the sign-posting that helps a reader follow your argument, but there's a limit to how many times in a row you have to make the same point. Maybe there's a whole chapter that would work just fine as its own, self-standing article. Out it goes. You can cite it in the book if you get it accepted by a journal soon enough. "As I have argued elsewhere," you say, citing yourself, then state the article's conclusion as though it were now self-evident.

You can also cut down the length by trimming the footnotes. The old standard, and one I still like to follow, was to give the full citation to a book or article the first time it's mentioned in a chapter, then just give the author's last name and a short version of the title for subsequent citations in the chapter. See if you have some places where you give the full citation more than once in a chapter and correct it. Whee, twenty extra words gone already! You can also leave out of the bibliography any work you cite only once and which is tangential to your main points, though of course you then need a full citation in the notes (and title your bibliography "Selected Bibliography"). Or you can adopt what is already the standard citation practice in some disciplines, and give all footnote citations in the form of, "Bouchard, 2022, p. 136." Then of course you have to have a complete bibliography.

But suppose you've done all this and your manuscript is still about ten thousand words longer than the press asked for? You can send it in anyway and hope they can find it in their hearts to take it as is, which they perhaps can. As I've said, they're used to dealing with academics (but shhh, don't tell them I told you this).

But realistically you need to make at least a good

faith effort to shrink the manuscript down further. Go through it one more time, eliminating unneeded phrases and words. You can easily dispense with, "When all of these arguments are taken together, it becomes clear that a closer examination of the source base is required," or, "Before beginning the analysis, it may seem appropriate to turn to some broader issues," or, "Given the complexity of the topic, it is necessary to give a fuller definition of terms before turning to the central argument." Anything flaccid can go. It will tighten up your prose and make the book more readable. At a certain point you may find you've made it a game with yourself, How many words can I eliminate from *this* page?

But suppose you have the opposite problem, the press asked for 80,000 words and you only have 60,000? Then you need to say more. Don't pad, don't triple space (that doesn't even work with freshmen), just realize that you have not carried your arguments far enough. Do so now. (Note that this is a very rare problem.)

As you make your final revisions, preparatory to sending your manuscript (in MS Word) back to the press, don't bother trying to make the manuscript look fancy. Just use one font throughout (probably Times New Roman or another plain-Jane serif font). Don't worry about widows and orphans (having a single line at the bottom or top of a page). Don't carefully add hyphens to make your righthand margin more even, just leave it ragged right. Certainly don't add running heads, though you should number your pages, starting with the title page as p. 1 (don't bother trying to get the front matter paginated as i, ii, iii, iv and so on, with p. 1 appearing on the first page of your Introduction). All this fancy formatting just gets in the way of the formatting the press themselves will be doing.

So you've rewritten your book, incorporating the readers' suggestions, tightened it up, polished it, and sent it off to the press, not so much later than they'd asked for it that you need to be embarrassed. In most cases, the editor will give it a quick read, to make sure you actually did what you promised to do, and send it to the copy-editors. Sometimes however the editor will have a brain wave that the second section of Chapter 2 would work great in the Introduction (for example). So you'll get it back *one more time.* Don't argue, don't obsess about it, just move the section and catch those final typos or incomplete footnotes you somehow missed. Now it really is ready for the copy-editors.

These are enormously careful and conscientious people who want your book to succeed. They will probably read your book more thoroughly and more carefully than anyone on the planet (except for you of course). (Or maybe a spouse.) It used to be that you would get back a pile of dog-eared pages with lots of scribbling in the margins, making it hard to recognize the beautifully printed pages you sent in. These days you will probably get your Word file back with Track Changes turned on and lots of little arrows and lines in different colors.

For me, this always causes temporary grumpiness (as you may have noticed, there are a certain number of grumpy stages in the glorious process of getting your book published). How could anyone try to mess with my perfect manuscript? I think. But by the next day I'm ready to see what the copy-editor has come up with. You will be too.

Part of their task is to correct your use of commas and make sure that your spelling, capitalization, and footnote format all correspond to what they call "house style" (you did remember to follow their guidelines this time, didn't you?). Just accept everything of this sort unless it radically changes your meaning. Sometimes the copy-editor will point out a sentence that makes no sense or a paragraph that appears to contradict what you said three pages earlier. Fix these problems and be glad someone noticed them before they reached the light of day.

At this point you can make a few amendments, like putting in the citation for that article of yours which has been published now (or at least accepted). If you realize you phrased something in an awkward way or said something you now realize was incorrect, you can make these small changes. Just don't try to rewrite everything. Copy-editors will tell you this happens too often.

Around this stage you will have to come up with illustrations, if your book is to have some, or at least some ideas for the cover. Any charts and graphs you are expected to create yourself. Maps are up to you to create (and pay the mapmaker). Images from manuscripts or stock photos may need to be negotiated with the copyright holder, and you will probably (not necessarily but probably) pay the license fees yourself. If you have high-resolution photos of your own that will do, use them. The press will pay for the cover art, but they won't pay you if they use your photo.

Also around this stage the press will finalize your title. You may have come up with a good title yourself, or they will help you come up with one. The main title can be something catchy, though again don't use "Love's Labour Lost" unless your book is about the wasted effort involved in love. But a Shakespearean phrase or something from the Bible can work, or just a few nouns. If the title doesn't make the book's content clear, add a subtitle, which will also reference the time and place covered (as in "….in eighteenth-century Spain"). Scholars in some countries, especially France, like long, leisurely titles, often starting with "A propos de" or something similar, but in the US and UK a fairly short and snappy title is preferred.

While checking the copy-editor's use of commas you'll realize you're sick of the book, almost as sick as you were of your dissertation. But finish going through it, send it back, and surprisingly soon you will get page proofs. Page proofs are enormously exciting. The pages look like a book! They have running heads and page numbers, the press's logo, your name on the title page, illustrations in place, and in short look like a real book written by a real author. That's you!

Go through the page proofs carefully. Find that one last typo that everyone missed. Make sure that in fixing the commas and incorporating your final emendations no new errors were introduced. It's still possible to make a few final changes, but the emphasis here is on "few." More than a handful, and the press is going to charge you (it says so in the contract).

While going through the page proofs, you are also expected to make an index. Note that while the deadline for sending your final manuscript in to the press was quite loose, the deadline for sending back the page proofs and the index is quite real. Your book has a slot all ready in the press's publication list for fall, and if you dawdle your book won't make it. You can hire a professional indexer or do it yourself.

Indexing can be tricky, because you don't want to index every person or thing mentioned, only the mentions that someone using the index would find useful. If your book is about Aquinas and women, you really don't need major entries for "Aquinas" or "women" (though you might have an index entry that directs to turning points in Aquinas's life). And sometimes you will want to include several different things under one entry that were discussed using different words, like "taxes," "tolls," and "excises." (Here you'd need a cross-reference: Tolls. *See* taxes.) The press will send you guidelines on preparing your index. Look at the indexes of other academic books you own, especially ones from that publisher, to get an idea of format and how it's done. I like doing my own indexing, because for one thing it's a final chance to catch errors ("What do I mean here, Philip I? Obviously I meant Philip II.")

Now you can't wait to see your book, but it won't appear for a while yet. Meanwhile the press will be sending you questionnaires and lists of things; they will indeed have started earlier. They will want your own brief statement of what the book's about, for the back cover and for the catalogue. They want a mini-bio of you and a nice head-shot. They want a list of good journals to send the book to for reviews. They suggest conferences where the book will be displayed or prizes for which your book might be eligible and ask if you have any to add. Their purpose in all of this is to make sure the book gets the attention it deserves. Yes, they really think your book is good and deserves attention. Otherwise they wouldn't be publishing it.

And then one day, when you're thinking of something else, a box arrives with your ten author copies. This is enormously exciting. The New Book Rule is that you're allowed to run up and down the hall yelling, show the book to everyone in sight, make them admire it and tell you all the parts they like best. You may get all hardcover books or a mix of hardcover and paperbacks, as the contract specified. Paperbacks will be printed if the press think the book might be used for "classroom adoption." All academic books these days also come out as ebooks, generally priced the same as the physical book. Give a hardback to your old dissertation adviser.

Congratulations! You've done it! You successfully turned your dissertation into a book.

Books by Constance Brittain Bouchard

MONOGRAPHS

Spirituality and Administration: The Role of the Bishop in Twelfth-Century Auxerre

Sword, Miter, and Cloister: Nobility and the Church in Burgundy, 980-1198

Life and Society in the Society in the West: Antiquity and the Middle Ages

Holy Entrepreneurs: Cistercians, Knights, and Economic Exchange in Twelfth-Century Burgundy

"Strong of Body, Brave and Noble": Chivalry and Society in Medieval France

"Those of My Blood": Constructing Noble Families in Medieval Francia

"Every Valley Shall Be Exalted": The Discourse of Opposites in Twelfth-Century Thought

Constance Brittain Bouchard

Rewriting Saints and Ancestors: Memory and Forgetting in France, 500-1200

Negotiation and Resistance: Peasant Agency in High Medieval France

CARTULARY EDITIONS

The Cartulary of Flavigny, 717-1113

The Cartulary of St.-Marcel-lès-Chalon, 779-1126

The Cartulary of Montier-en-Der, 666-1129

Three Cartularies from Thirteenth-Century Auxerre

The Cartulary-Chronicle of Bèze

EDITED VOLUME

Knights in History and Legend

WRITING AS C. DALE BRITTAIN

<u>The Royal Wizard of Yurt</u>

A Bad Spell in Yurt

The Wood Nymph and the Cranky Saint

The Lost Girls and the Kobold

Mage Quest

Beneath the Wizards' Tower

The Witch and the Cathedral

Daughter of Magic

A Long Way 'Til November

Is This Apocalypse Necessary?

<u>Yurt, the Next Generation</u>

The Starlight Raven

An Autumn Haunting

The Sapphire Ring

The Ill-Born Prince

<u>Epic Fantasy</u>

Shadow of the Wanderers

Count Scar [with Robert A Bouchard]

Heretic Wind [with Robert A Bouchard]

<u>Medieval Tales Retold</u>

The Sign of the Rose

Ashes of Heaven

The Knight of the Short Nose

<u>History</u>

Positively Medieval: Life and Society in the Middle Ages

Contested Christmas

<u>Miscellany</u>

How I Survived Junior High [YA fiction]

Know Your Self-Publishing [DIY advice]